Sudoku
For
Kids

by

Anne Brown

VERY EASY

Puzzle One

4	2	3	1
1	3	2	4
3	4	1	2
2	1	4	3

Puzzle Two

2	3	4	1
4	1	2	3
3	4	1	2
1	2	3	4

Puzzle Three

1	4	2	3
3	2	4	1
4	3	1	2
2	1	3	4

Puzzle Four

3	1	4	2
2	4	1	3
1	2	3	4
4	3	2	1

Puzzle Five

1	2	3	4
3	4	1	2
4	1	2	3
2	3	4	1

Puzzle Six

2	3	4	1
4	1	3	2
3	2	1	4
1	4	2	3

Puzzle Seven

2	4	3	1
3	1	4	2
1	3	2	4
4	2	1	3

Puzzle Eight

2	3	4	1
4	1	2	3
3	2	1	4
1	4	3	2

Puzzle Nine

3	2	1	4
4	1	2	3
1	3	4	2
2	4	3	1

Puzzle Ten

1	2	4	3
4	3	1	2
3	4	2	4
2	1	3	1

Puzzle Eleven

1	3	2	4
4	2	1	3
3	1	4	2
2	4	3	1

Puzzle Twelve

1	2	3	4
4	3	2	1
2	4	1	3
3	1	2	4

Puzzle Thirteen

1	2	4	3
4	3	1	2
3	1	2	4
2	4	3	1

Puzzle Fourteen

4	3	1	2
1	2	4	3
3	1	2	4
2	4	3	1

Puzzle Fifteen

4	1	2	3
3	2	1	4
2	3	4	1
1	4	3	2

Puzzle Sixteen

2	3	4	1
4	1	2	3
1	2	3	4
3	4	1	2

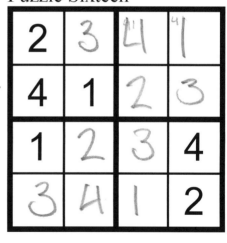

Puzzle Seventeen

1	4	2	3
3	2	4	1
4	3	1	2
2	1	3	4

Puzzle Eighteen

2	1	4	3
4	3	2	1
3	4	1	2
1	2	3	4

Puzzle Nineteen

1	3	4	2
2	4	3	1
4	1	2	3
3	2	1	4

Puzzle Twenty

1	4	2	3
3	2	4	1
2	3	1	4
4	1	3	2

Puzzle Twenty-one

2	1	4	3
3	4	2	1
1	2	3	4
4	3	1	2

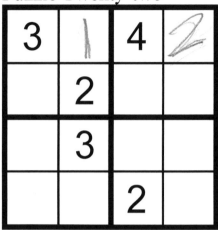

Puzzle Twenty-two

3	1	4	2
	2		
	3		
		2	

Puzzle Twenty-three

	1		
		3	
1			2
4			

Puzzle Twenty-four

	1		
			1
		2	
4			3

Puzzle Twenty-five

	3		
1	4	3	
		1	3
		2	

EASY

Puzzle Twenty-six

		3	1
			2
2			
	4		

Puzzle Twenty-seven

3		1	
4			
		4	
			2

Puzzle Twenty-eight

3			1
4		2	

Puzzle Twenty-eight

3			
		2	
	1		4

Puzzle Thirty

			2
		1	
3			
		4	

Puzzle Thirty-one

4			
		2	
	1		3

Puzzle Thirty-two

	1	4	
2		3	

Puzzle Thirty-three

	1		3
	3	2	1

Puzzle Thirty-four

		3	
2			
			4
4		2	

Puzzle Thirty-five

		1	2
4			2

Puzzle Thirty-six

4		3	
	1		2

Puzzle Thirty-seven

3	4		
		1	4

Puzzle Thirty-eight

		2	1
		3	
	2	1	

Puzzle Thirty-nine

2			3
			4
1			

Puzzle Forty

3	4		
		3	1

Puzzle Forty-one

	1		
		4	
	3		1

Puzzle Forty-two

		1	
3		4	
	3		
4			

Puzzle Forty-three

			3
1			
2	1		

Puzzle Forty-four

3			4
		1	
2	4		

Puzzle Forty-five

	1	3	
	4		
	3	1	

Puzzle Forty-six

4			2
	2	3	
			3

Puzzle Forty-seven

		3	4
			1
	4		

Puzzle Forty-eight

		1	
	1		
	2		
		4	

Puzzle Forty-nine

3	4		
1	3	4	

Puzzle Fifty

2			
	4		3
		4	1

Medium Easy

Puzzle Fifty-one

	6	3		2	
3				4	
		6			5
		5	4	3	
		2		6	4

Puzzle Fifty-two

	1		6		
4				3	
	2				
	3	5			1
5	4				2

Puzzle Fifty-three

	5	1			
		3			
		4	6	3	
		5			
	4			3	1
	2				

Puzzle Fifty-four

6	2			3	
4				2	5
		2	3		
		1			
3	4	5		1	
1			2	5	

Puzzle Fifty-five

	2		3	5	
6			5		2
		4	2		
	6	3		2	5
		5	4		
	3			4	

Puzzle Fifty-six

		3		6	
		5	6	4	
		4			
	3				2
2				1	
	4	2			6

Puzzle Fifty-seven

1			3		2
		6			
				1	6
	5		4	2	
				5	
2	1		5		

Puzzle Fifty-eight

				5	4
5	2		6		
6	5	2			3
	3				
			4	6	

Puzzle Fifty-nine

			6	1	
		4		2	
5		2		6	
2	1				
4	5				
		1		4	

Puzzle Sixty

2		5		6	
3	4		1		2
6					4
1					
			2	3	

Puzzle Sixty-one

					3
					2
	5	4			
1			6		
		1			
2		6		3	

Puzzle Sixty-two

			5	3	6
	4				2
				1	
2					3
		2	3	6	
	6				1

Puzzle Sixty-three

	1		3		
	2	1		3	6
			4	2	
1				4	
3			6	1	2
2		5			

Puzzle Sixty-four

		2		4	3
		3			1
			1		
4					
		1	2		
			6	5	

Puzzle Sixty-five

	1			6	
	5	2		1	4
4					2
6		4			5
				4	
1					

Puzzle Sixty-six

6	2				
5		6			3
	4	2			
	3		6		
1		4			6
			5		1

Puzzle Sixty-seven

		2			4
	2			1	6
			3		5
		3	5		
		6	1	4	2

Puzzle Sixty-eight

1		6	5		
4			3		6
			2		
6	1			3	2
			1	6	4
					1

Puzzle Sixty-nine

2		1			
	4	5			
			2	5	4
3	1			4	
				3	
4	6			2	1

Puzzle Seventy

3					
1	2	6	3		5
6	4				1
		1	5	2	
			6		4
2					

Puzzle Seventy-one

		5	1	3	
		3			1
		4		2	
3		1	4		2
	4				
6		2	3		

Puzzle Seventy-two

	6	3		4	5
3	5	6			
			1	3	
2					
5		4		1	

Puzzle Seventy-three

				2	4
	2		4		
		2		6	3
4		6	3		
	1		5		

Puzzle Seventy-four

1	2				
		2		6	
	5				
5		1		4	
2		5		1	3
	1	3			5

Puzzle Seventy-five

	4	6	3		
	5		2		
					4
			4	6	3
2	3	5			
		3			5

Medium Harder

Puzzle Seventy-six

			5	1	6
	6				2
		2	1		
	3			4	
			3		

Puzzle Seventy-seven

				4	
			2		
6				5	
	6				
	1	4		6	
		1			5

Puzzle Seventy-eight

		6	4		
3			2		6
			1	5	2
5				6	

Puzzle Seventy-nine

	3		2		
1	2		3		
4		2		6	
		6			
			1		4

Puzzle Eighty

			4		
				1	
	4	5		2	
				5	6
	1				
2		6			

Puzzle Eighty-one

	6	2	3		
					4
		5			
				2	
	2				
3				1	

Puzzle Eighty-two

				5	
4	6				
			3		
	1			3	
		6		2	
			2		

Puzzle Eighty-three

6			4		5
	1				
3					
	2		5	1	
		2		6	

Puzzle Eighty-four

					1
3			6		2
6					
		1	5		
					3
	2			1	

Puzzle Eighty-five

	4			2	6
	2				
		6			
			4		1
					3
1		3			

Puzzle Eighty-six

6				4	
		5			
			1	6	2
	2				6
4					
		3		5	

Puzzle Eighty-seven

			1		5
				2	
		4			
5	2				1
	1			3	6
	6				

Puzzle Eighty-eight

6					
			2		
	5	4		1	
		6	4		
	3				5
			3		

Puzzle eighty-nine

		5		3	1
		6	2		
	4	3		6	
3					
6		2			

Puzzle Ninety

			3	1	5
	4		6		
	1				3
					4
6	3				

Puzzle Ninety-one

1				6	
			3		4
3		6	4		
	6				
	4		5		

Puzzle Ninety-two

	2				
	6	1			5
		3			
6					4
			4		2
				1	

Puzzle Ninety-three

				1	
	3	2			
			6		
5		4			
					4
		5		2	6

Puzzle Ninety-four

	1				
	3			4	
6			1		
				3	
	4	5			
		6	3		

Puzzle Ninety-five

					3
1					5
			2	1	
	2		5	6	
			3		
			1		

Puzzle Ninety-six

	4				
					2
	5				1
3			5		
			1		
		4		6	

Puzzle Ninety-seven

	1				
3					6
	2				4
4		1			
		6			
				4	3

Puzzle Ninety-eight

	3		4		
5		3			
					6
			1		
			6		3
				5	1

Puzzle Ninety-nine

	6		2		
4	5		6		
		6		5	1
				3	
			4		

Puzzle One hundred

				3	
	2	6			
	6		5		
			4		2
	4				1

Harder

One Hundred and one

8	6	5				4		
9								
	3		8	6		5		1
		6				3	4	
		4	1	7				5
7	2		3	4				6
	8	9	2	1		7	6	
				8				2
	1		4		7		3	

One Hundred and two

3			6	5	8	2	4	
			1			7		
6	5		7	4		8		
		8				6		
5	9	3						
				2			8	
1			5				7	
8						3		1
	4	7		9		5		

One Hundred and three

		3		2	6	1		5
8								
1		2	5			7	4	9
			2	3	7		5	1
9			6		8		7	2
		1						3
5	8			9	2	6		4
				4		3		
			8		5	2	9	

One Hundred and four

		4		7	6		1	3
1			5			9		7
	7					5		2
5	4		9					6
	9		8	3	7		5	4
				5	7			
		3						
				9			7	
2	8			6	4			5

One Hundred and five

			1	9				3
1		3	2	6	4			
	6		8					
5	8		3				2	4
	1		9	8	2		3	5
3							7	1
	4	1	6	3				
			7			1		6
		9		5	1	3		

One Hundred and six

		4	7	5				
7							2	4
				1	4			
		3	5		7			
9		2		3		5		
	4			6	2			
	5			2				
4	8				3	2	5	
	1	7	8	9				

One Hundred and seven

8			3		6			
		2		7		1		6
		1	8					3
			4	7		6		
6			5	8				
	2	7	9		8	5		
5		6	7			2	9	
1			4	6	2			7

One Hundred and eight

	3	5	7	2				
8	7	1	9		4		2	6
4	2		1	6				5
7	6		3	9		2		4
1	4				2	9		
				4			6	
				1				
3						6	4	
2	5	6		3	7	1		

One Hundred and nine

3		4		2				6
5								7
		6	8	4	9			3
8		2						
				9		4		8
9				8		2	6	1
	6					1		
4	9	1	5			7	3	
	3	8			1	6	9	5

One Hundred and ten

		1						
				8	3	6	9	
6		8	1			7	2	5
8							6	
		9	8	2		1		7
	6				7	9		2
7	1			3				6
5					4		7	9
4				7	2			

One Hundred and eleven

	3	6		5				7
			2				5	3
				1	3	4		
4		3				1		
		2			1		6	
5		1		9	2	7		8
		5						
				3	5	8		
8	1	7		2				5

One Hundred and twelve

		4	2	3				7
7		3		6	9	8		
9					8		2	
	5	2	6	8			3	
6	7				3		4	8
1	3	8	9	5				
			7	9	2			
2		5	3	1				4
	6				5	2	9	1

One Hundred and thirteen

	4		2	9	5		8	
								9
	9	5	8			4		
2	1							
3		9		5	6			1
			4					8
4	3	1		7				2
7				2		3		4
		6		3	4		7	

One Hundred and fourteen

		5	8		7	2		
	4	2		3		9		8
8		6	1		9	7		
2	1			8				6
	5		9		3	8		
	7	6	5	2				1
		3				2		
	6		2				4	
			4	9	5	6		

One Hundred and fifteen

8	2			6		7	5	4
9					5		1	
		6	7		4		8	9
		2	3	4	1			
	5		6	9		3		
	6			5				7
2	4					9	3	
	1		4	7	9			6
	8							5

One Hundred and sixteen

			4			1		
6				2	1	9	4	
	3		5	9		2	8	7
	1	6		4			2	
	4	9		6		3		
		7			3	6		
8	6		2	1			5	9
	5				4		1	
		4		8		7	3	2

One Hundred and seventeen

		6			3			8
	3		1				6	9
			7	9		5		
2	4		9		1		8	
9				7	4			6
			8			7		
		3				8		1
8		9	4		7			2
	2	5		1				7

One Hundred and eighteen

			7	8				
	8		6		5			
		6	3			2		
1		7		6		4	3	
	6				9		8	
			5		3			6
			3	7	6	4		
	2		4	5		8		
				1	8		5	7

One Hundred and nineteen

9	1	4				2		8
5		3	8				1	4
	8						3	9
				7	3	4		2
7		8				9		
	3				4		6	7
	9		6					
		7		3		8		
	6	5				3	2	

One Hundred and twenty

			2			9	5	
	7	8		3	9	2		6
			4	8				
	3			1			2	
7			6		4			3
8				2	3			1
1			6	2	7			
		7	9		5			
		5		1				2

One Hundred and twenty-one

		5	4				3	
			7				4	9
2	3			1			5	7
	2	6				5		
8		3			1	7		
	1	7				3	9	
	8		2	7	3	4		
3		1						
7				4		6		

One Hundred and twenty-two

9		4		1			3	
		3		8		6		
	5	8			6		4	7
4		6	1	5	2	9		3
	1	9	8					
3				6	9	4		
				2	1			8
8	9					3		
				3		1	7	

One Hundred and twenty-three

		4	1	6		2		
5	9	3					1	6
		1			5	4		
			9	3		5		4
	4			2				
	3	2			1			9
1	8	9		5	6		4	
4		7		9	3	6	5	
			2	1		9	8	7

One Hundred and twenty-four

3	9	5		6	2	1		7
		1	5	4	7			9
7	6							
	2		6		5	9		
			2	7		6		
4		6	1					3
5		9			8			
	2	4			3	8	9	1
8					6		5	

Very Hard

One Hundred and twenty-five

		1			3			
		9	2			7	1	5
9	4		8		5		3	6
	6	1	7	2		5		
	3				9			
5		9	4			8	2	
	7	2	3					
	5					8		
1	6		2					9

One Hundred and twenty-six

6		2						8
	7	3				2		5
				7	9			
	5				9		3	
			8					2
	7			1	5			
	6	5					1	
	1							
	8	4						3

One Hundred and twenty-seven

8			6					4
					7	8		3
		7		4				
				3				9
3								
9						6	2	
		8			4	1		
2							9	
	5	3	1				8	

One Hundred and twenty-eight

				5	1			
8	7					2		6
			2				3	
	5	2	1			7	6	
				4				
	1	3						
		8	2	1				
1					3			5
	3	4	6					

One Hundred and twenty-nine

9						5	4	
		5			9	1		8
	2							
	9			5	2			
			1				6	
8							9	
			8	6	4	2		
7						4		
5	8			1				

One Hundred and thirty

9	7				3			6
		1	8			9	3	
					4			
			6	3			1	2
		8				4	6	7
				5				3
	6					1		8
		9	2	4				
					6			

One Hundred and thirty-one

6	3			9		8		
								2
7		1	2				3	
		3	5				7	
			1	8				
2	4					1		3
		5	6		2	7		
4						9		
								6

One Hundred and thirty-two

1	5			3	6			
		8	7	2	9			
3		2						
			8					
		4	9	3				
	2		5					4
	7	9						
			6	1				5
	6		8		2			

One Hundred and thirty-three

				9	2	7	3	
							4	
1		3				5	6	
	7				8	4		
			9					
8	3			2				
	9			7		1		
		6			5			
	5		2	4				3

One Hundred and thirty-four

		8						9
9	4		6	7				
		2				4		
		3	2		9	7		8
		5						
	9		1				5	
4				3	6	8		
8				2			9	
	5		8	1		6		

One Hundred and thirty-five

6					3			8
		8		4				5
	5							1
					7			
	3		4					9
9					8		2	
				2	6	1		3
				8			7	6
		4	3		1			

One Hundred and thirty-six

4								
		7	6			2		
5					3	8		
7	9			1	5		4	
							9	
		6	8				3	
				7				5
	2		5		1	7		
				6	8	3		

One Hundred and thirty-seven

			9					
	1			2			8	
		3		8			4	
			5					2
		7					9	1
		1	2		6		3	8
3		4		7				
		5						
2			4		5	9		

One Hundred and thirty-eight

					8	2	9	6
		4		2	6	8	1	
						4		3
		5		8				9
		6						
			1	9	5	3		
			8		4			
3	7							
					1		5	4

One Hundred and thirty-nine

		7		4				
				8		6	9	
1	2				7			
		4					8	
			6		5	7	2	
			5					
		6			2			
	4		1		5			9
2	5		4					

One Hundred and forty

5			9	1	4			
3						4		
	8		5	6				7
	1					8		
			7	9				6
6			3					4
		2			7		5	
						3		1

One Hundred and forty-one

		6						
7				8				
					7	5	1	
			1	3		4		
8		9					6	
						7		5
	1		4				9	6
6				7		2		
	5	3			8			

One Hundred and forty-two

			4					5
		6	5			2	7	
		1						9
7			9					
		5						4
4	6			3		2		
			3		6			
3			8			4		2
	2					1		

One Hundred and forty-three

	4							
3		8						2
6			3					4
		2			8			3
	6	9			3			5
	3		4	6				1
			7		5			9
		8						
		5		2		7		

One Hundred and forty-four

								9
	5		8	9				6
			7	4	2			
		7	5					
		5				2		
3			1	2	9			8
					1	8	2	
7		1			9		4	
		3						

One Hundred and forty-five

	1							5
	2	6		3				
4				1		2		
		3			8		9	
		5				3		
	9				3			1
		8						
	6		7			1		
3				9	6		5	8

One Hundred and forty-six

	6						7	1
			3	1				9
9						2		8
8		3			9			
				5	2	3		
			7					
	1						6	7
4							9	5
				8		4		

One Hundred and forty-seven

	6	2		4				
	9		2					
			9	7				
5						2		
		8			4		6	
	2						1	8
1		6	8		2		5	3
	5		1					7
	3							

One Hundred and forty-eight

					4			
2		1						8
3			1	5				
5		8				2	6	
1						3		
6			4			1		7
						8	1	
	3	5					4	9
			7					6

One Hundred and forty-nine

4			3		8			
8	7	6	2					
						5		
		1			4			
3	6					2		
		4		3		7		1
9								
			6	2	5			
	8	7				1		

One Hundred and fifty

		8						5
		7			6			9
4				3				
		4			7	5		
	9				5	8		
				1	3	9		
	6	9		5		4		
	1				9			
7			6					

Solutions

Puzzle one

4	2	3	1
1	3	2	4
3	4	1	2
2	1	4	3

Puzzle two

2	3	4	1
4	1	2	3
3	4	1	2
1	2	3	4

Puzzle three

1	4	2	3
3	2	4	1
4	3	1	2
2	1	3	4

Puzzle four

3	1	4	2
2	4	1	3
1	2	3	4
4	3	2	1

Puzzle five

1	2	3	4
3	4	1	2
4	1	2	3
2	3	4	1

Puzzle six

2	3	4	1
4	1	3	2
3	2	1	4
1	4	2	3

Puzzle seven

2	4	3	1
3	1	4	2
1	3	2	4
4	2	1	3

Puzzle eight

2	3	4	1
4	1	2	3
3	2	1	4
1	4	3	2

Puzzle nine

3	2	1	4
4	1	2	3
1	3	4	2
2	4	3	1

Puzzle ten

1	2	4	3
4	3	1	2
3	4	2	1
2	1	3	4

Puzzle eleven

1	3	2	4
4	2	1	3
3	1	4	2
2	4	3	1

Puzzle twelve

1	2	3	4
4	3	2	1
2	4	1	3
3	1	4	2

Puzzle thirteen

1	2	4	3
4	3	1	2
3	1	2	4
2	4	3	1

Puzzle fourteen

4	3	1	2
1	2	4	3
3	1	2	4
2	4	3	1

Puzzle fifteen

4	1	2	3
3	2	1	4
2	3	4	1
1	4	3	2

Puzzle sixteen

2	3	4	1
4	1	2	3
1	2	3	4
3	4	1	2

Puzzle seventeen

1	4	2	3
3	2	4	1
4	3	1	2
2	1	3	4

Puzzle eighteen

2	1	4	3
4	3	2	1
3	4	1	2
1	2	3	4

Puzzle nineteen

1	3	4	2
2	4	3	1
4	1	2	3
3	2	1	4

Puzzle twenty

1	4	2	3
3	2	4	1
2	3	1	4
4	1	3	2

Puzzle twenty-one

2	1	4	3
3	4	2	1
1	2	3	4
4	3	1	2

Puzzle twenty-two

3	1	4	2
4	2	3	1
2	3	1	4
1	4	2	3

Puzzle twenty-three

3	1	2	4
2	4	3	1
1	3	4	2
4	2	1	3

Puzzle twenty-four

3	1	4	2
2	4	3	1
1	3	2	4
4	2	1	3

Puzzle twenty-five

2	3	4	1
1	4	3	2
4	2	1	3
3	1	2	4

Puzzle twenty-six

4	2	3	1
3	1	4	2
2	3	1	4
1	4	2	3

Puzzle twenty-seven

3	2	1	4
4	1	2	3
2	3	4	1
1	4	3	2

Puzzle twenty-eight

1	4	3	2
3	2	4	1
4	1	2	3
2	3	1	4

Puzzle twenty-nine

1	2	4	3
3	4	1	2
4	3	2	1
2	1	3	4

Puzzle thirty

4	1	3	2
2	3	1	4
3	4	2	1
1	2	4	3

Puzzle thirty-one

4	2	3	1
1	3	2	4
3	4	1	2
2	1	4	3

Puzzle thirty-two

3	1	4	2
4	2	1	3
2	4	3	1
1	3	2	4

Puzzle thirty-three

3	4	1	2
2	1	4	3
1	2	3	4
4	3	2	1

Puzzle thirty-four

1	4	3	2
2	3	4	1
3	2	1	4
4	1	2	3

Puzzle thirty-five

2	4	3	1
3	1	2	4
1	2	4	3
4	3	1	2

Puzzle thirty-six

1	3	2	4
4	2	3	1
2	4	1	3
3	1	4	2

Puzzle thirty-seven

1	2	4	3
3	4	2	1
2	3	1	4
4	1	3	2

Puzzle thirty-eight

3	4	2	1
2	1	3	4
1	3	4	2
4	2	1	3

Puzzle thirty-nine

2	4	1	3
3	1	2	4
4	2	3	1
1	3	4	2

Puzzle forty

3	4	1	2
2	1	4	3
1	3	2	4
4	2	3	1

Puzzle forty-one

3	4	1	2
2	1	3	4
1	2	4	3
4	3	2	1

Puzzle forty-two

2	4	1	3
3	1	4	2
1	3	2	4
4	2	3	1

Puzzle forty-three

4	2	1	3
1	3	4	2
2	1	3	4
3	4	2	1

Puzzle forty-four

3	1	2	4
4	2	1	3
1	3	4	2
2	4	3	1

Puzzle forty-five

2	1	3	4
3	4	2	1
1	2	4	3
4	3	1	2

Puzzle forty-six

4	3	1	2
1	2	3	4
3	4	2	1
2	1	4	3

Puzzle forty-seven

4	3	1	2
2	1	3	4
3	2	4	1
1	4	2	3

Puzzle forty-eight

2	4	1	3
3	1	2	4
4	2	3	1
1	3	4	2

Puzzle forty-nine

2	1	3	4
3	4	2	1
1	3	4	2
4	2	1	3

Puzzle fifty

2	3	1	4
1	4	2	3
4	1	3	2
3	2	4	1

Puzzle fifty-one

1	2	4	6	5	3
4	6	3	5	2	1
3	5	1	2	4	6
2	4	6	3	1	5
6	1	5	4	3	2
5	3	2	1	6	4

Puzzle fifty-two

2	6	3	5	1	4
3	1	4	6	2	5
4	5	2	1	3	6
1	2	6	4	5	3
6	3	5	2	4	1
5	4	1	3	6	2

Puzzle fifty-three

3	5	1	6	4	2
4	6	2	3	1	5
2	1	5	4	6	3
1	3	4	5	2	6
5	4	6	2	3	1
6	2	3	1	5	4

Puzzle fifty-four

6	2	4	5	3	1
4	3	6	1	2	5
5	1	2	3	4	6
2	5	1	4	6	3
3	4	5	6	1	2
1	6	3	2	5	4

Puzzle fifty-five

1	2	6	3	5	4
6	4	1	5	3	2
3	5	4	2	1	6
4	6	3	1	2	5
2	1	5	4	6	3
5	3	2	6	4	1

Puzzle fifty-six

4	1	3	2	6	5
3	2	5	6	4	1
5	6	4	1	2	3
6	3	1	4	5	2
2	5	6	3	1	4
1	4	2	5	3	6

Puzzle fifty-seven

1	6	5	3	4	2
4	2	6	1	3	5
5	3	4	2	1	6
6	5	1	4	2	3
3	4	2	6	5	1
2	1	3	5	6	4

Puzzle fifty-eight

3	6	1	2	5	4
1	4	5	3	2	6
5	2	4	6	3	1
6	5	2	1	4	3
4	3	6	5	1	2
2	1	3	4	6	5

Puzzle fifty-nine

3	2	5	6	1	4
1	6	4	3	2	5
5	4	2	1	6	3
2	1	3	4	5	6
4	5	6	2	3	1
6	3	1	5	4	2

Puzzle sixty

2	1	5	4	6	3
3	4	6	1	5	2
5	6	2	3	4	1
6	2	3	5	1	4
1	3	4	6	2	5
4	5	1	2	3	6

Puzzle sixty-one

6	2	5	1	4	3
4	1	3	6	5	2
3	5	4	2	1	6
1	3	2	4	6	5
5	6	1	3	2	4
2	4	6	5	3	1

Puzzle sixty-two

1	2	4	5	3	6
6	4	3	1	5	2
5	3	6	2	1	4
2	5	1	6	4	3
4	1	2	3	6	5
3	6	5	4	2	1

Puzzle sixty-three

6	1	2	3	5	4
4	2	1	5	3	6
5	3	6	4	2	1
1	6	3	2	4	5
3	5	4	6	1	2
2	4	5	1	6	3

Puzzle sixty-four

6	1	2	5	4	3
2	5	3	4	6	1
3	4	6	1	2	5
4	2	5	3	1	6
5	6	1	2	3	4
1	3	4	6	5	2

Puzzle sixty-five

2	1	5	4	6	3
3	5	2	6	1	4
4	6	1	3	5	2
6	2	4	1	3	5
5	3	6	2	4	1
1	4	3	5	2	6

Puzzle sixty-six

6	2	5	3	1	4
5	1	6	4	2	3
3	4	2	1	6	5
4	3	1	6	5	2
1	5	4	2	3	6
2	6	3	5	4	1

Puzzle sixty-seven

1	5	2	6	3	4
3	2	5	4	1	6
4	6	1	3	2	5
6	1	4	2	5	3
2	4	3	5	6	1
5	3	6	1	4	2

Puzzle sixty-eight

1	2	6	5	4	3
4	5	1	3	2	6
3	6	4	2	1	5
6	1	5	4	3	2
5	3	2	1	6	4
2	4	3	6	5	1

Puzzle sixty-nine

2	5	1	4	6	3
6	4	5	3	1	2
1	3	6	2	5	4
3	1	2	6	4	5
5	2	4	1	3	6
4	6	3	5	2	1

Puzzle seventy

3	5	4	1	6	2
1	2	6	3	4	5
6	4	5	2	3	1
4	6	1	5	2	3
5	3	2	6	1	4
2	1	3	4	5	6

Puzzle seventy-one

4	2	5	1	3	6
5	6	3	2	4	1
1	3	4	6	2	5
3	5	1	4	6	2
2	4	6	5	1	3
6	1	2	3	5	4

Puzzle seventy-two

1	6	3	2	4	5
3	5	6	4	2	1
4	2	5	1	3	6
2	4	1	5	6	3
6	1	2	3	5	4
5	3	4	6	1	2

Puzzle seventy-three

1	3	5	6	2	4
6	2	3	4	5	1
5	4	2	1	6	3
3	6	1	2	4	5
4	5	6	3	1	2
2	1	4	5	3	6

Puzzle seventy-four

1	2	6	3	5	4
3	4	2	5	6	1
6	5	4	1	3	2
5	3	1	2	4	6
2	6	5	4	1	3
4	1	3	6	2	5

Puzzle seventy-five

1	4	6	3	5	2
3	5	4	2	1	6
6	2	1	5	3	4
5	1	2	4	6	3
2	3	5	6	4	1
4	6	3	1	2	5

Puzzle seventy-six

4	2	3	5	1	6
1	5	6	2	3	4
3	6	1	4	5	2
5	4	2	1	6	3
2	3	5	6	4	1
6	1	4	3	2	5

Puzzle seventy-seven

3	5	6	1	4	2
1	4	5	2	3	6
6	2	3	4	5	1
5	6	2	3	1	4
2	1	4	5	6	3
4	3	1	6	2	5

Puzzle seventy-eight

1	2	6	4	3	5
3	5	1	2	4	6
4	6	3	5	2	1
2	4	5	6	1	3
6	3	4	1	5	2
5	1	2	3	6	4

Puzzle seventy-nine

5	4	1	6	3	2
6	3	4	2	1	5
1	2	5	3	4	6
4	1	2	5	6	3
3	5	6	4	2	1
2	6	3	1	5	4

Puzzle eighty

3	2	1	4	6	5
5	6	3	2	1	4
1	4	5	6	2	3
4	3	2	1	5	6
6	1	4	5	3	2
2	5	6	3	4	1

Puzzle eighty-one

4	6	2	3	5	1
2	5	1	6	3	4
1	3	5	4	6	2
6	1	4	5	2	3
5	2	3	1	4	6
3	4	6	2	1	5

Puzzle eighty-two

1	3	4	6	5	2
4	6	2	5	1	3
5	2	1	3	6	4
2	1	5	4	3	6
3	4	6	1	2	5
6	5	3	2	4	1

Puzzle eighty-three

2	4	5	6	3	1
6	3	1	4	2	5
5	1	3	2	4	6
3	6	4	1	5	2
4	2	6	5	1	3
1	5	2	3	6	4

Puzzle eighty-four

2	5	3	4	6	1
3	1	5	6	4	2
6	4	2	1	3	5
4	3	1	5	2	6
1	6	4	2	5	3
5	2	6	3	1	4

Puzzle eighty-five

3	4	1	5	2	6
6	2	4	3	1	5
5	1	6	2	3	4
2	3	5	4	6	1
4	6	2	1	5	3
1	5	3	6	4	2

Puzzle eighty-six

6	1	2	3	4	5
2	4	5	6	1	3
3	5	4	1	6	2
5	2	1	4	3	6
4	3	6	5	2	1
1	6	3	2	5	4

Puzzle eighty-seven

2	4	3	1	6	5
1	3	5	6	2	4
6	5	4	2	1	3
5	2	6	3	4	1
4	1	2	5	3	6
3	6	1	4	5	2

Puzzle eighty-eight

6	1	3	2	5	4
3	4	1	5	2	6
2	5	4	6	1	3
5	2	6	4	3	1
4	3	2	1	6	5
1	6	5	3	4	2

Puzzle eighty-nine

2	6	5	4	3	1
4	5	1	3	2	6
1	3	6	2	5	4
5	4	3	1	6	2
3	2	4	6	1	5
6	1	2	5	4	3

Puzzle ninety

2	6	4	3	1	5
1	4	5	6	3	2
3	5	1	2	4	6
4	1	6	5	2	3
5	2	3	1	6	4
6	3	2	4	5	1

Puzzle ninety-one

4	2	5	6	3	1
1	3	4	2	6	5
6	5	1	3	2	4
3	1	6	4	5	2
5	6	2	1	4	3
2	4	3	5	1	6

Puzzle ninety-two

1	2	4	5	6	3
3	6	1	2	4	5
4	5	3	6	2	1
6	3	2	1	5	4
5	1	6	4	3	2
2	4	5	3	1	6

Puzzle ninety-three

6	4	3	5	1	2
1	3	2	4	6	5
2	5	1	6	4	3
5	6	4	2	3	1
3	2	6	1	5	4
4	1	5	3	2	6

Puzzle ninety-four

4	1	3	5	6	2
5	3	2	6	4	1
6	2	4	1	5	3
2	6	1	4	3	5
3	4	5	2	1	6
1	5	6	3	2	4

Puzzle ninety-five

2	5	1	6	4	3
1	6	3	4	2	5
4	3	5	2	1	6
3	2	4	5	6	1
6	1	2	3	5	4
5	4	6	1	3	2

Puzzle ninety-six

2	4	1	3	5	6
1	3	5	6	4	2
6	5	2	4	3	1
3	2	6	5	1	4
4	6	3	1	2	5
5	1	4	2	6	3

Puzzle ninety-seven

6	1	4	2	3	5
3	4	5	1	2	6
5	2	3	6	1	4
4	5	1	3	6	2
2	3	6	4	5	1
1	6	2	5	4	3

Puzzle ninety-eight

1	3	6	4	2	5
5	6	3	2	1	4
4	2	1	5	3	6
3	5	4	1	6	2
2	1	5	6	4	3
6	4	2	3	5	1

Puzzle ninety-nine

1	6	5	2	4	3
4	5	3	6	1	2
3	2	4	1	6	5
2	4	6	3	5	1
6	1	2	5	3	4
5	3	1	4	2	6

Puzzle one hundred

5	1	4	2	3	6
4	2	6	3	1	5
3	6	1	5	2	4
1	3	5	4	6	2
6	5	2	1	4	3
2	4	3	6	5	1

Puzzle one hundred and one

8	6	5	7	9	1	4	2	3
9	4	1	5	3	2	6	7	8
2	3	7	8	6	4	5	9	1
1	5	6	9	2	8	3	4	7
3	9	4	1	7	6	2	8	5
7	2	8	3	4	5	9	1	6
5	8	9	2	1	3	7	6	4
4	7	3	6	8	9	1	5	2
6	1	2	4	5	7	8	3	9

Puzzle one hundred and two

3	7	1	6	5	8	2	4	9
9	8	4	1	2	3	7	5	6
6	5	2	7	4	9	8	1	3
4	2	8	9	1	5	6	3	7
5	9	3	8	6	7	1	2	4
7	1	6	4	3	2	9	8	5
1	3	9	5	8	6	4	7	2
8	6	5	2	7	4	3	9	1
2	4	7	3	9	1	5	6	8

Puzzle one hundred and three

4	7	3	9	2	6	1	8	5
8	5	9	7	4	1	3	2	6
1	6	2	5	8	3	7	4	9
6	4	8	2	3	7	9	5	1
9	3	5	6	1	8	4	7	2
7	2	1	4	5	9	8	6	3
5	8	7	3	9	2	6	1	4
2	9	6	1	7	4	5	3	8
3	1	4	8	6	5	2	9	7

Puzzle one hundred and four

9	5	4	2	7	6	8	1	3
1	2	6	5	8	3	9	4	7
3	7	8	4	1	9	5	6	2
5	4	7	9	2	1	3	8	6
6	9	1	8	3	7	2	5	4
8	3	2	6	4	5	7	9	1
7	6	3	1	5	8	4	2	9
4	1	5	3	9	2	6	7	8
2	8	9	7	6	4	1	3	5

Puzzle one hundred and five

2	7	8	1	9	5	4	6	3
1	5	3	2	6	4	7	9	8
9	6	4	8	7	3	5	1	2
5	8	6	3	1	7	9	2	4
4	1	7	9	8	2	6	3	5
3	9	2	5	4	6	8	7	1
7	4	1	6	3	8	2	5	9
8	3	5	7	2	9	1	4	6
6	2	9	4	5	1	3	8	7

Puzzle one hundred and six

1	2	4	7	5	9	6	3	8
7	9	5	3	8	6	1	2	4
6	3	8	2	1	4	7	9	5
8	6	3	5	4	7	9	1	2
9	7	2	1	3	8	5	4	6
5	4	1	9	6	2	3	8	7
3	5	6	4	2	1	8	7	9
4	8	9	6	7	3	2	5	1
2	1	7	8	9	5	4	6	3

Puzzle one hundred and seven

8	4	9	3	1	6	2	7	5
3	5	2	9	7	4	1	8	6
7	6	1	8	2	5	9	4	3
9	8	5	1	4	7	3	6	2
6	1	3	2	5	8	7	9	4
4	2	7	6	9	3	8	5	1
5	3	6	7	8	1	4	2	9
2	7	4	5	3	9	6	1	8
1	9	8	4	6	2	5	3	7

Puzzle one hundred and eight

6	3	5	7	2	8	4	9	1
8	7	1	9	5	4	3	2	6
4	2	9	1	6	3	8	7	5
7	6	8	3	9	5	2	1	4
1	4	3	6	7	2	9	5	8
5	9	2	8	4	1	7	6	3
9	8	4	2	1	6	5	3	7
3	1	7	5	8	9	6	4	2
2	5	6	4	3	7	1	8	9

Puzzle one hundred and nine

3	8	4	7	2	5	9	1	6
5	2	9	6	1	3	8	4	7
1	7	6	8	4	9	5	2	3
8	4	2	1	5	6	3	7	9
6	1	3	2	9	7	4	5	8
9	5	7	3	8	4	2	6	1
7	6	5	9	3	2	1	8	4
4	9	1	5	6	8	7	3	2
2	3	8	4	7	1	6	9	5

Puzzle one hundred and ten

9	7	1	2	6	5	8	3	4
2	4	5	7	8	3	6	9	1
6	3	8	1	4	9	7	2	5
8	2	7	4	9	1	5	6	3
3	5	9	8	2	6	1	4	7
1	6	4	3	5	7	9	8	2
7	1	2	9	3	8	4	5	6
5	8	3	6	1	4	2	7	9
4	9	6	5	7	2	3	1	8

Puzzle one hundred and eleven

2	3	6	8	5	4	9	1	7
1	4	8	2	7	9	6	5	3
7	5	9	6	1	3	4	8	2
4	8	3	5	6	7	1	2	9
9	7	2	3	8	1	5	6	4
5	6	1	4	9	2	7	3	8
3	9	5	1	4	8	2	7	6
6	2	4	7	3	5	8	9	1
8	1	7	9	2	6	3	4	5

Puzzle one hundred and twelve

5	8	4	2	3	1	9	6	7
7	2	3	4	6	9	8	1	5
9	1	6	5	7	8	4	2	3
4	5	2	6	8	7	1	3	9
6	7	9	1	2	3	5	4	8
1	3	8	9	5	4	6	7	2
8	4	1	7	9	2	3	5	6
2	9	5	3	1	6	7	8	4
3	6	7	8	4	5	2	9	1

Puzzle one hundred and thirteen

6	4	3	2	9	5	1	8	7
8	7	2	3	4	1	5	6	9
1	9	5	8	6	7	4	2	3
2	1	4	9	8	3	7	5	6
3	8	9	7	5	6	2	4	1
5	6	7	4	1	2	9	3	8
4	3	1	5	7	8	6	9	2
7	5	8	6	2	9	3	1	4
9	2	6	1	3	4	8	7	5

Puzzle one hundred and fourteen

1	9	5	8	4	7	2	6	3
7	4	2	5	3	6	9	1	8
8	3	6	1	2	9	7	5	4
2	1	3	7	8	4	5	9	6
6	5	4	9	1	3	8	7	2
9	8	7	6	5	2	4	3	1
4	7	9	3	6	8	1	2	5
5	6	8	2	7	1	3	4	9
3	2	1	4	9	5	6	8	7

Puzzle one hundred and fifteen

8	2	1	9	6	3	7	5	4
9	7	4	8	2	5	6	1	3
5	3	6	7	1	4	2	8	9
7	9	2	3	4	1	5	6	8
1	5	8	6	9	7	3	4	2
4	6	3	2	5	8	1	9	7
2	4	7	5	8	6	9	3	1
3	1	5	4	7	9	8	2	6
6	8	9	1	3	2	4	7	5

Puzzle one hundred and sixteen

9	2	5	4	7	8	1	6	3
6	7	8	3	2	1	9	4	5
4	3	1	5	9	6	2	8	7
3	1	6	7	4	9	5	2	8
5	4	9	8	6	2	3	7	1
2	8	7	1	5	3	6	9	4
8	6	3	2	1	7	4	5	9
7	5	2	9	3	4	8	1	6
1	9	4	6	8	5	7	3	2

Puzzle one hundred and seventeen

5	9	6	2	4	3	1	7	8
7	3	2	1	8	5	4	6	9
1	8	4	7	9	6	5	2	3
2	4	7	9	6	1	3	8	5
9	5	8	3	7	4	2	1	6
3	6	1	8	5	2	7	9	4
6	7	3	5	2	9	8	4	1
8	1	9	4	3	7	6	5	2
4	2	5	6	1	8	9	3	7

Puzzle one hundred and eighteen

2	3	9	7	8	1	5	6	4
4	8	1	6	2	5	9	7	3
5	7	6	3	9	4	2	1	8
1	5	7	8	6	2	4	3	9
3	6	2	1	4	9	7	8	5
9	4	8	5	7	3	1	2	6
8	1	5	9	3	7	6	4	2
7	2	3	4	5	6	8	9	1
6	9	4	2	1	8	3	5	7

Puzzle one hundred and nineteen

9	1	4	3	5	6	2	7	8
5	7	3	8	9	2	6	1	4
6	8	2	4	1	7	5	3	9
1	5	6	9	7	3	4	8	2
7	4	8	2	6	1	9	5	3
2	3	9	5	8	4	1	6	7
3	9	1	6	2	8	7	4	5
4	2	7	1	3	5	8	9	6
8	6	5	7	4	9	3	2	1

Puzzle one hundred and twenty

3	1	4	2	7	6	9	5	8
5	7	8	1	3	9	2	4	6
6	9	2	4	8	5	1	3	7
4	3	9	8	1	7	6	2	5
7	2	1	6	5	4	8	9	3
8	5	6	9	2	3	4	7	1
1	4	3	5	6	2	7	8	9
2	6	7	3	9	8	5	1	4
9	8	5	7	4	1	3	6	2

Puzzle one hundred and twenty-one

9	7	5	4	6	2	1	3	8
1	6	8	7	3	5	2	4	9
2	3	4	9	1	8	6	5	7
4	2	6	3	9	7	5	8	1
8	9	3	6	5	1	7	2	4
5	1	7	8	2	4	3	9	6
6	8	9	2	7	3	4	1	5
3	4	1	5	8	6	9	7	2
7	5	2	1	4	9	8	6	3

Puzzle one hundred and twenty-two

9	6	4	2	1	7	8	3	5
7	2	3	5	8	4	6	1	9
1	5	8	3	9	6	2	4	7
4	7	6	1	5	2	9	8	3
5	1	9	8	4	3	7	6	2
3	8	2	7	6	9	4	5	1
6	3	7	4	2	1	5	9	8
8	9	1	6	7	5	3	2	4
2	4	5	9	3	8	1	7	6

Puzzle one hundred and twenty-three

8	7	4	1	6	9	2	3	5
5	9	3	4	8	2	7	1	6
2	6	1	3	7	5	4	9	8
6	1	8	9	3	7	5	2	4
9	4	5	6	2	8	1	7	3
7	3	2	5	4	1	8	6	9
1	8	9	7	5	6	3	4	2
4	2	7	8	9	3	6	5	1
3	5	6	2	1	4	9	8	7

Puzzle one hundred and twenty-four

3	9	5	8	6	2	1	4	7
2	8	1	5	4	7	3	6	9
7	6	4	3	9	1	5	2	8
1	2	7	6	3	5	9	8	4
9	3	8	2	7	4	6	1	5
4	5	6	1	8	9	2	7	3
5	1	9	7	2	8	4	3	6
6	7	2	4	5	3	8	9	1
8	4	3	9	1	6	7	5	2

Puzzle one hundred and twenty-five

2	5	1	7	6	3	4	9	8
6	3	8	9	2	4	7	1	5
9	4	7	8	1	5	2	3	6
4	8	6	1	7	2	9	5	3
7	2	3	5	8	9	6	4	1
5	1	9	4	3	6	8	2	7
8	7	2	3	9	1	5	6	4
3	9	5	6	4	7	1	8	2
1	6	4	2	5	8	3	7	9

Puzzle one hundred and twenty-six

6	9	2	1	5	4	3	7	8
1	7	3	8	9	6	2	4	5
5	8	4	3	2	7	9	6	1
8	5	6	2	4	9	1	3	7
4	1	9	7	8	3	6	5	2
2	3	7	6	1	5	4	8	9
3	6	5	9	7	2	8	1	4
9	4	1	5	3	8	7	2	6
7	2	8	4	6	1	5	9	3

Puzzle one hundred and twenty-seven

8	2	1	6	3	5	9	7	4
6	4	9	2	1	7	8	5	3
5	3	7	8	4	9	6	2	1
1	8	2	7	6	3	5	4	9
3	6	4	9	5	2	7	1	8
9	7	5	4	8	1	3	6	2
7	9	8	5	2	4	1	3	6
2	1	6	3	7	8	4	9	5
4	5	3	1	9	6	2	8	7

Puzzle one hundred and twenty-eight

3	2	6	8	5	1	7	9	4
8	7	1	4	3	9	2	5	6
9	4	5	7	2	6	1	3	8
4	5	2	1	9	7	6	8	3
6	8	9	3	4	2	5	7	1
7	1	3	5	6	8	9	4	2
5	9	8	2	1	4	3	6	7
1	6	7	9	8	3	4	2	5
2	3	4	6	7	5	8	1	9

Puzzle one hundred and twenty-nine

9	1	8	7	2	3	5	4	6
3	7	5	6	4	9	1	2	8
4	2	6	5	8	1	9	7	3
6	9	7	3	5	2	8	1	4
2	4	3	1	9	8	7	6	5
8	5	1	4	7	6	3	9	2
1	3	9	8	6	4	2	5	7
7	6	2	9	3	5	4	8	1
5	8	4	2	1	7	6	3	9

Puzzle one hundred and thirty

9	7	4	5	1	3	2	8	6
6	5	1	8	7	2	9	3	4
8	2	3	9	6	4	7	5	1
4	9	7	6	3	8	5	1	2
5	3	8	1	2	9	4	6	7
2	1	6	4	5	7	8	9	3
7	6	2	3	9	5	1	4	8
3	8	9	2	4	1	6	7	5
1	4	5	7	8	6	3	2	9

Puzzle one hundred and thirty-one

6	3	2	4	9	5	8	1	7
9	8	4	7	3	1	5	6	2
7	5	1	2	6	8	4	3	9
1	6	3	5	2	4	9	7	8
5	7	9	1	8	3	6	2	4
2	4	8	9	7	6	1	5	3
3	9	5	6	4	2	7	8	1
4	2	6	8	1	7	3	9	5
8	1	7	3	5	9	2	4	6

Puzzle one hundred and thirty-two

1	5	7	9	3	6	4	2	8
6	4	8	5	7	2	9	3	1
3	9	2	4	1	8	6	5	7
7	3	5	8	2	4	1	6	9
8	1	4	6	9	3	5	7	2
9	2	6	1	5	7	3	8	4
2	7	9	3	4	5	8	1	6
4	8	3	2	6	1	7	9	5
5	6	1	7	8	9	2	4	3

Puzzle one hundred and thirty-three

5	4	8	6	9	2	7	3	1
9	6	7	5	1	3	8	4	2
1	2	3	7	8	4	5	6	9
2	7	9	3	6	8	4	1	5
6	1	4	9	5	7	3	2	8
8	3	5	4	2	1	9	7	6
3	9	2	8	7	6	1	5	4
4	8	6	1	3	5	2	9	7
7	5	1	2	4	9	6	8	3

Puzzle one hundred and thirty-four

5	7	8	3	4	2	1	6	9
9	4	1	6	7	8	5	2	3
6	3	2	5	9	1	4	8	7
1	6	3	2	5	9	7	4	8
2	8	5	4	6	7	9	3	1
7	9	4	1	8	3	2	5	6
4	2	7	9	3	6	8	1	5
8	1	6	7	2	5	3	9	4
3	5	9	8	1	4	6	7	2

Puzzle one hundred and thirty-five

6	7	2	5	1	3	4	9	8
1	9	8	6	4	2	7	3	5
4	5	3	8	7	9	2	6	1
8	1	6	2	9	7	3	5	4
2	3	7	4	6	5	8	1	9
9	4	5	1	3	8	6	2	7
5	8	9	7	2	6	1	4	3
3	2	1	9	8	4	5	7	6
7	6	4	3	5	1	9	8	2

Puzzle one hundred and thirty-six

4	6	8	1	5	2	9	7	3
9	3	7	6	8	4	2	5	1
5	1	2	9	7	3	8	6	4
7	9	3	2	1	5	6	4	8
8	4	1	7	3	6	5	9	2
2	5	6	8	4	9	1	3	7
6	8	9	3	2	7	4	1	5
3	2	4	5	9	1	7	8	6
1	7	5	4	6	8	3	2	9

Puzzle one hundred and thirty-seven

8	6	2	9	5	4	1	7	3
4	1	9	7	2	3	6	8	5
7	5	3	6	8	1	2	4	9
9	3	8	5	1	7	4	6	2
6	2	7	3	4	8	5	9	1
5	4	1	2	9	6	7	3	8
3	9	4	1	7	2	8	5	6
1	7	5	8	6	9	3	2	4
2	8	6	4	3	5	9	1	7

Puzzle one hundred and thirty-eight

1	5	3	4	7	8	2	9	6
9	7	4	3	2	6	8	1	5
6	8	2	1	9	5	4	7	3
3	1	5	2	8	7	6	4	9
2	9	6	5	4	3	7	8	1
7	4	8	6	1	9	5	3	2
5	6	1	8	3	4	9	2	7
4	3	7	9	5	2	1	6	8
8	2	9	7	6	1	3	5	4

Puzzle one hundred and thirty-nine

6	8	7	9	4	3	1	2	5
4	3	5	2	8	1	6	9	7
1	2	9	6	5	7	8	3	4
5	6	4	7	2	9	3	8	1
8	9	1	3	6	4	5	7	2
3	7	2	5	1	8	9	4	6
9	1	6	8	7	2	4	5	3
7	4	8	1	3	5	2	6	9
2	5	3	4	9	6	7	1	8

Puzzle one hundred and forty

5	2	8	9	1	4	7	6	3
1	6	4	2	7	3	5	8	9
3	9	7	8	5	6	4	1	2
4	8	9	5	6	1	2	3	7
7	1	6	4	3	2	8	9	5
2	5	3	7	9	8	1	4	6
6	7	1	3	8	5	9	2	4
9	3	2	1	4	7	6	5	8
8	4	5	6	2	9	3	7	1

Puzzle one hundred and forty-one

3	2	5	6	1	4	9	7	8
7	9	1	5	8	2	6	3	4
4	6	8	3	9	7	5	1	2
5	7	2	1	3	6	4	8	9
8	4	9	7	2	5	3	6	1
1	3	6	8	4	9	7	2	5
2	1	7	4	5	3	8	9	6
6	8	4	9	7	1	2	5	3
9	5	3	2	6	8	1	4	7

Puzzle one hundred and forty-two

2	9	3	6	4	7	1	8	5
8	4	6	1	5	9	3	2	7
5	7	1	2	8	3	6	4	9
7	8	2	9	1	4	5	3	6
1	3	5	7	6	2	8	9	4
4	6	9	5	3	8	2	7	1
9	1	4	3	2	6	7	5	8
3	5	7	8	9	1	4	6	2
6	2	8	4	7	5	9	1	3

Puzzle one hundred and forty-three

5	4	1	6	2	8	9	3	7
3	9	8	4	1	7	6	5	2
6	2	7	9	3	5	1	8	4
1	7	4	2	5	9	8	6	3
2	6	9	1	8	3	7	4	5
8	3	5	7	4	6	2	9	1
4	8	6	3	7	1	5	2	9
7	5	2	8	9	4	3	1	6
9	1	3	5	6	2	4	7	8

Puzzle one hundred and forty-four

6	7	2	5	1	3	8	4	9
1	5	4	8	9	2	3	7	6
9	3	8	6	7	4	2	1	5
2	1	7	4	5	8	6	9	3
8	9	5	7	3	6	4	2	1
3	4	6	1	2	9	7	5	8
5	6	9	3	4	7	1	8	2
7	8	1	2	6	5	9	3	4
4	2	3	9	8	1	5	6	7

Puzzle one hundred and forty-five

8	1	7	9	6	2	4	3	5
5	2	6	8	3	4	9	1	7
4	3	9	5	1	7	8	2	6
1	7	3	4	5	8	6	9	2
6	8	5	1	2	9	3	7	4
2	9	4	6	7	3	5	8	1
7	5	8	3	4	1	2	6	9
9	6	2	7	8	5	1	4	3
3	4	1	2	9	6	7	5	8

Puzzle one hundred and forty-six

3	6	4	2	9	8	5	7	1
5	8	2	3	1	7	6	4	9
9	7	1	5	4	6	2	3	8
8	5	3	4	6	9	7	1	2
7	4	9	1	5	2	3	8	6
1	2	6	7	8	3	9	5	4
2	1	8	9	3	5	4	6	7
4	3	7	6	2	1	8	9	5
6	9	5	8	7	4	1	2	3

Puzzle one hundred and forty-seven

7	6	2	3	4	8	5	9	1
3	9	5	2	1	6	8	7	4
4	8	1	5	9	7	6	3	2
5	7	3	6	8	1	4	2	9
9	1	8	7	2	4	3	6	5
6	2	4	9	3	5	7	1	8
1	4	6	8	7	2	9	5	3
8	5	9	1	6	3	2	4	7
2	3	7	4	5	9	1	8	6

Puzzle one hundred and forty-eight

9	5	7	2	8	4	6	3	1
2	6	1	7	9	3	4	5	8
3	4	8	1	5	6	9	7	2
5	9	3	8	1	7	2	6	4
1	7	4	9	6	2	3	8	5
6	8	2	4	3	5	1	9	7
7	2	6	5	4	9	8	1	3
8	3	5	6	2	1	7	4	9
4	1	9	3	7	8	5	2	6

Puzzle one hundred and forty-nine

4	1	5	3	7	8	6	9	2
8	7	6	2	5	9	3	1	4
2	3	9	1	4	6	8	5	7
7	2	1	9	6	4	5	8	3
3	6	8	5	1	7	2	4	9
5	9	4	8	3	2	7	6	1
9	5	2	7	8	1	4	3	6
1	4	3	6	2	5	9	7	8
6	8	7	4	9	3	1	2	5

Puzzle one hundred and fifty

9	3	8	1	7	4	2	6	5
1	2	7	5	8	6	4	3	9
4	5	6	9	3	2	1	7	8
6	8	4	2	9	7	3	5	1
3	9	1	4	6	5	7	8	2
5	7	2	8	1	3	6	9	4
2	6	9	3	5	1	8	4	7
8	1	3	7	4	9	5	2	6
7	4	5	6	2	8	9	1	3